Brock Purdy : From Mr. Irrelevant To Mr. Incredible

How Brock Purdy Became A Star Quarterback

Chad C. Love

Brock Purdy

Table Of Contents

Brock Purdy

INTRODUCTION

You can't just call Brock Purdy an NFL star. Coming out of high school, he wasn't a highly sought-after prospect. His draft position was not in the first round. For his inaugural season, not even a lot of playing was anticipated of him. In actuality, he was the last selection in the 2022 NFL Draft, which gave him the questionable moniker "Mr. Irrelevant". However, Purdy disproved everyone with his incredible ascent from obscurity to celebrity, winning two NFC West championships in a row and making an appearance in the Super Bowl with the San Francisco 49ers.

You will discover Purdy's story in this book, from a small-town youngster in Arizona to an NFL phenomenon and record-breaking quarterback at Iowa State. You'll learn how his perseverance, self-assurance, and love of the game helped him overcome hardship, criticism, and uncertainty. A behind-the-scenes look at his character, connections, and influence on teammates, coaches, and supporters will also be provided.

Beyond being a sporting biography, Brock Purdy: From Mr. Irrelevant To Mr. Incredible is more. It is a motivational tale of tenacity, grit, and achievement. It is evidence of the value of having self-confidence and pursuing your goals. It pays homage to one of the NFL's most improbable but enduring heroes.

Background of Mr. Irrelevant Title

The San Francisco 49ers' quarterback, Brock Purdy, has had an outstanding NFL career so far. He wasn't, however, always thought of as a standout performer. The moniker "Mr. Irrelevant" was bestowed upon him since he was the last selection in the 2022 NFL Draft.

Paul Salata, a former NFL player and coach, created the phrase "Mr. Irrelevant" when he invited the draft's last choice and his family to a week-long party in Newport Beach, California. The Lowsman Trophy, a spoof of the Heisman Trophy that features a player fumbling a football, is presented at the event along with a trip to Disneyland, a golf tournament, a roast, and other activities.

After spending four seasons as an Iowa State player, Purdy was selected with the 262nd and last choice in the 2022 NFL Draft. The 49ers chose him since they already had two quarterbacks on the squad: Jimmy Garoppolo, who led the team to the 2020 Super Bowl, and Trey Lance, the third overall choice in the 2021 NFL Draft. However, destiny had other ideas. Purdy was supposed to be a practice squad player or a backup.

Lance had a right ankle injury in the second game of the 2022 season that prevented him from playing for the remainder of the season. Purdy was the team's sole healthy quarterback until Garoppolo injured his foot on the first drive of the 13th game of the season. With 18 of 23 passes for 236 yards and two scores, Purdy took over and guided the 49ers to a 33-17 victory against the Miami Dolphins.

In his first NFL start, Purdy showed no signs of slowing down, defeating Tom Brady and the Tampa Bay Buccaneers 35-7 while running for a score and passing for 287 yards. In his first NFL start, he became the first quarterback to defeat Brady, and in the regular season, he became the first Mr. Irrelevant to complete a forward pass and toss a touchdown pass.

With a 10-0 record as a starter at the end of his first year, Purdy led the 49ers to the NFC West championship and the NFC Championship

Game, where they were defeated by the Philadelphia Eagles. With a passing rating of 106.7, Purdy completed his throws for 3,021 yards, 24 touchdowns, and six interceptions. In addition, he was awarded the Pepsi NFL Rookie of the Year and the NFL Offensive Rookie of the Year.

Purdy has been even more effective in his second season, helping the 49ers to a 5-0 start and the best record in the NFL. With a passer rating of 118.9, he has completed 15 touchdown passes, two interceptions, and 1,543 yards of passing. He might win MVP since he is regarded as one of the league's greatest young quarterbacks.

It's not necessary to be Mr. Irrelevant to be irrelevant, as Purdy has shown. He has shown that anything is achievable if you have enthusiasm, confidence, and hard effort. He is now revered by the 49ers and the NFL as a leader, hero, and beloved by the fans. He is now Mr. Incredible instead of Mr. Irrelevant.

CHAPTER 1 : EARLY YEARS AND FAMILY BACKGROUND

Football player Brock Purdy is a rising star for the San Francisco 49ers. He plays quarterback. Shawn and Carrie Purdy welcomed him into the world on December 27, 1999, in Queen Creek, Arizona. His mother co-owns a pool company with him, and his father played in minor league baseball for eight seasons. Brock has a younger brother named Chubba who plays quarterback at Florida State University and an older sister named Whittney who played softball at Southeastern University.

At Gilbert, Arizona's Perry High School, where he began playing football, Brock developed into one of the state's top quarterbacks. In 2016 and 2017, he guided his team to two straight 6A Division AIA State Championship games, which they ultimately lost to Chandler High School. In terms of throwing yards (14,539), passing touchdowns (161), and total touchdowns (186), he established many state records.

Although Brock had great high school statistics, he was not extensively sought by collegiate schools. Only a select few universities, including Alabama, Texas A&M, and Iowa State, extended offers to him. He made the decision to play for the Iowa State Cyclones, and he excelled throughout his time in college. In addition to holding the school records for most throwing yards (11,021), most passing touchdowns (93), and most overall touchdowns (114), he was selected to the first team of the Big 12 twice.

Brock joined the 2022 NFL Draft and became Mr. Irrelevant when the San Francisco 49ers picked him with the last choice. He was the third-string quarterback at the beginning of the season, but injuries to Jimmy Garoppolo and Trey Lance gave him the opportunity to play. He helped the 49ers secure a division championship and advance to the NFC Championship Game by winning all five of the regular-season games he started. In 2023, he maintained his starting position and set league records for passer rating, passing yards, and passing touchdowns. In addition, he surpassed the team record for throwing yards in a single season and was nominated to his first Pro Bowl.

Early life and family history have moulded Brock Purdy into an exceptional football player who has triumphed over several obstacles. Many young players who want to play in the NFL look up to him as an inspiration.

Purdy's Early Interest In Football

It was clear from an early age that Brock Purdy was interested in football. His father was a former minor league baseball pitcher, and his siblings were football and softball players. He grew up in a household that was passionate about sports. He played a lot of sports, including golf, baseball, basketball, and soccer, but his favourite was football.

When he was five years old, he began playing football, and his dream position was quarterback. He practised tossing the ball in their backyard with his father and brother, and he looked up to NFL players like Aaron Rodgers, Tom Brady, and Peyton Manning. He also studied from the greatest by watching a lot of football games on TV.

He displayed his abilities and leadership qualities when playing youth football with the

Queen Creek Bulldogs. At Perry High School, where he played football till the end, he developed into one of Arizona's top quarterbacks. He broke many state records and led his team to two state championship games. Along with these accolades, he was also awarded the Ed Doherty Award and the Gatorade Arizona Player of the Year.

Early football fandom gave Brock Purdy the drive and will to follow his ambition of becoming an NFL player. He triumphed over several obstacles and skepticisms along his journey, showcasing his exceptional skills as a quarterback at Iowa State and the San Francisco 49ers. Many young players who love the game as much as he does look up to him.

High School Achievements And Challenges

During his time at Perry High School, Brock Purdy faced a number of difficulties in addition to notable successes.

Successes:

Brock Purdy

Performance of the year : Purdy was an exceptional quarterback who broke several school records. He ran for 1,106 yards and 10 touchdowns in addition to throwing for 4,410 yards and 57 touchdowns in only his final year. He was named the Arizona Gatorade Player of the Year as a result of his achievements.

Leading the squad to victory : In 2015 and 2016, Perry High School advanced to the AIA 6A State Championship game under Purdy's direction. Even though they were unsuccessful in capturing the title both times, Purdy's skill and guidance were crucial to their achievement.

Beyond the field of play : In addition to being a standout athlete, Purdy was a devoted learner and well-liked member of the campus community. He participated in a number of extracurricular activities and kept up a strong GPA.

Difficulties:

Brock Purdy

Participating in a challenging league:
Perry High School faced other formidable
teams with exceptional players in a tough
conference. Purdy was forced by this rivalry
to sharpen his abilities and fortify himself as
a player.

Overcoming ailments: Throughout his high
school career, Purdy missed a few games
because of injuries. Even though they were
difficult, these defeats eventually
strengthened and determined him.

Recruiting challenges : Purdy wasn't
extensively pursued by big universities
despite his great numbers and awards. It was
perhaps because of his diminutive size in
comparison to other quarterbacks. Purdy
persisted however, and in the end he was
awarded a scholarship to Iowa State
University, where he had a prosperous
collegiate career.

Throughout his high school career, Brock
Purdy overcame obstacles and achieved
extraordinary achievement. His
achievements on and off the football field

Brock Purdy

were made possible by his skill, commitment, and fortitude.

CHAPTER 2 : COLLEGE RECRUITMENT JOURNEY

The quarterback for the San Francisco 49ers, Brock Purdy, was selected with the last choice in the 2022 NFL Draft. He played professionally for a while before having an outstanding collegiate career at Iowa State. Purdy was a three-star recruit out of Gilbert, Arizona's Perry High School, where he earned the 2017 Arizona Gatorade Player of the Year title and established other records.

At least thirteen offers from different universities, including Alabama, Texas A&M, Boise State, and others, were extended to Purdy. He did not, however, make a commitment to any school until late January 2018, by which time most of the best quarterbacks had signed with other teams.

Purdy thought that the coaching staff at Iowa State prioritised him and demonstrated to him how he could work within their system to advance the team, which is why he selected Iowa State over the other universities. He also enjoyed the team's and the school's culture and environment.

After enrolling at Iowa State in February 2018, Purdy rapidly rose to the position of starting quarterback and guided the Cyclones to an 8-4 record and an Alamo Bowl appearance as a rookie. In addition to setting other school marks, he won the Big 12 Offensive Freshman of the Year award. For the following three seasons, Purdy kept up his impressive play at Iowa State, setting records for throwing yards, touchdowns, completion percentage, and total offence. In 2020, he also guided the Cyclones to their first Fiesta Bowl triumph and their first trip to the Big 12 Championship Game.

Despite being predicted as a mid-round draft selection, Purdy made the decision to stay for his senior year in 2021. He finished as a candidate for the Johnny Unitas Golden Arm Award, earned All-Big 12 recognition, and led the Cyclones to a 9–4 record and another bowl victory.

Despite being one of the most accomplished and successful quarterbacks in college football history when he entered the 2022 NFL Draft, Purdy's lack of stature, arm power, and mobility caused many clubs to pass on him. The 49ers picked him with the 262nd overall choice, making him the last player chosen and earning the moniker Mr. Irrelevant.

Surprising a lot of people, Purdy joined the 49ers as the backup quarterback to Jimmy Garoppolo and Trey Lance. When Garoppolo and Lance were sidelined in December 2022, he was given the opportunity to start. In his first two games, he did a good job guiding the 49ers to a victory over the Rams and a narrow defeat to the Cardinals.

Purdy is anticipated to start all of the 49ers' 2022 games as they attempt to secure a postseason berth and contend for the Super Bowl. In his limited NFL career, he has shown composure, accuracy, and leadership, and he has gained the respect and confidence of his coaches and teammates.

Purdy's decision-making process

The San Francisco 49ers quarterback Brock Purdy has shown exceptional decision-making and execution abilities on the field. His physical characteristics, his coaching background and experience, and his aptitude for field analysis and defensive anticipation all play a role in his decision-making process.

Among the elements influencing his decision-making process are:

- The ball's quality and the surrounding weather. Wet balls and other conditions that make it more difficult to hold and toss the ball correctly have caused Purdy difficulties.

- The blocking strategy and the pass protection. Purdy depends on his offensive line to provide him with enough time and room to throw the ball and make his reads. In addition, he must modify his choices in light of the formation and his available back alternatives.

- The possible damage to his elbow. During a game against the Packers, Purdy took a hit to the elbow, which could have had an impact on his confidence and effectiveness in certain plays.

- The coverage and the defensive approach. Purdy needs to read the alignment and habits of the defender, predict their moves and responses. Considering the routes and the distance between his receivers, he must act quickly and decisively.

Along with certain experts and fans, Purdy's decision-making method has received accolades from his coaches and teammates. He has shown the ability to execute daring yet spectacular plays in addition to difficult and accurate throws. In crucial moments, he has shown fortitude and leadership by inspiring his squad to several victories via comebacks.

Some commentators have also questioned Purdy's decision-making process, pointing out his dubious choices and wasted chances. He has been charged as being erratic, unsure of himself, or careless at times, which has led to sacks, fumbles, or missed passes.

Purdy's decision-making process is a multifaceted, dynamic phenomena that depends on a wide range of elements. Since it varies depending on the setting and conclusion of each play, it is difficult to assess or describe. Purdy has acknowledged that he sometimes errs or regrets his decisions, but he also makes an effort to grow as a player and learn from them. One of the most important components of Purdy's performance and quarterback potential is his decision-making process, which will be put to the test in the next NFC championship game against the Detroit Lions.

Choosing Iowa State University

American football quarterback Brock Purdy is presently a member of the San Francisco 49ers football team. In the 2022 NFL Draft, he was selected by the 49ers with the last selection, making him the year's Mr. Irrelevant. Purdy played collegiate football for the Iowa State Cyclones from 2018 to 2021 before entering the NFL. After Seneca Wallace in 2003, he was the first quarterback from Iowa State to be picked.

Purdy turned down offers from more established football colleges like Texas A&M and Alabama in favour of attending Iowa State. He decided what he did for a few straightforward reasons. He first sensed that Iowa State prioritised him and really wanted him. He was grateful when half of the coaching staff came to see him at home and gave him advice on how to advance the program. Second, he likes Iowa State's atmosphere and culture. With the players, coaches, and spectators, he felt at ease. Playing in the very competitive Big 12 league, which features high-scoring offences, was another challenge he enjoyed. Third, he put his faith and instincts to the test. He believed that Iowa State was the ideal fit for him and prayed about his choice.

Purdy made a smart decision by attending Iowa State. In his four years there, he broke many school records and was named starter as a freshman. In 2020, he guided the Cyclones to their first Fiesta Bowl triumph and three straight bowl victories. In addition, he was named to the Big 12 first team twice, and he concluded as the conference's all-time leader in total offence. Head coach Matt Campbell guided him as he matured, praising Purdy's toughness, leadership, and competitiveness. Purdy's time in college gave him excellent preparation for the NFL, where he has already shown he has what it takes to be a starting member of the 49ers.

CHAPTER 3 : MR. IRRELEVANT TO MR. INCREDIBLE

Brock Purdy's transformation from Mr. Irrelevant to Mr. Incredible is an inspiring tale of skill, tenacity, and will. The San Francisco 49ers chose Purdy as the 262nd overall choice with their last pick in the 2022 NFL Draft. He earned the moniker "Mr. Irrelevant," a moniker bestowed upon the last draft selection since 1976.

Jimmy Garoppolo and Trey Lance were the 49ers' starting quarterbacks, with Purdy coming in third. Until Garoppolo fractured his foot on the first drive of the game against the Miami Dolphins on December 4, 2023, he did not witness any action. Purdy took over and threw for 198 yards and two touchdowns to lead the 49ers to victory, 33-17.

In the second game of the season, Lance had an ankle injury that ended his season. As a result, Purdy started for the 49ers. His composure, precision, and agility won over the coaches and supporters. With a passer rating of

95.6 at the end of the regular season, he ended with 3,721 passing yards, 28 touchdowns, and 10 interceptions. Six touchdowns and 421 yards were gained with his run.

The 49ers finished 13-3 under Purdy's direction and won the NFC West division. As the 49ers beat the Kansas City Chiefs 31–24 in Super Bowl LVII, he also made history as the first Mr. Irrelevant to start a postseason game and win a championship. After passing for 287 yards and three touchdowns and rushing for 54 yards and one more, Purdy was crowned the MVP of the Super Bowl.

Purdy won many awards for his outstanding season, including NFL Most Valuable Player, NFL Comeback Player of the Year, and NFL Offensive Player of the Year. He was named to the All-Pro team and the Pro Bowl as well. As a rookie, he became the first player in NFL history to win both the MVP award for the Super Bowl and the MVP award for the whole league.

Purdy's popularity and sponsorship agreements increased as a result of his success. He made several appearances in periodicals, talk programs, and advertisements. Additionally, he was chosen to be the cover athlete for Madden NFL 25, the popular video game franchise's 25th anniversary edition. The media and his followers gave him the moniker Mr. Incredible, which was appropriate given his remarkable turnaround from Mr. Irrelevant.

Notable moments in Purdy's college career

From 2018 to 2021, quarterback Brock Purdy was a member of the Iowa State Cyclones collegiate football team. He is an NFL player now with the San Francisco 49ers. On October 6, 2018, Purdy played his first game as a freshman, guiding Iowa State to an unexpected 48–42 win against No. 25 Oklahoma State. In addition to running for 84 yards and a score, he completed 18 of 23 throws for 318 yards and four touchdowns. Because of his efforts, he was awarded the Big 12 Newcomer of the Week.

Purdy broke the school record on November 16, 2019, when he passed for 492 yards in a single game against Kansas. In addition, he tied a school record with six touchdown passes from the air. In a 41–31 victory, he completed 29 of

42 passes and added 55 running yards. Because of his effort, he was voted the Big 12 Offensive Player of the Week.

Purdy guided Iowa State to its first Big 12 Championship Game appearance on December 19, 2020, against Oklahoma, ranked No. 10. In a 27-21 defeat, he ran for 38 yards and a score in addition to throwing for 322 yards and a touchdown, but he also threw three interceptions. For the 2020 campaign, he was selected to the All-Big 12 First Team.

Purdy assisted Iowa State in defeating No. 25 Oregon in the Fiesta Bowl, the inaugural New Year's Six bowl game, on January 2, 2021. In a 34–17 victory, he rushed for a score in addition to completing 20 of 29 passes for 156 yards and a touchdown. For his efforts, he was voted the Fiesta Bowl Offensive MVP.

On November 13, 2021, Purdy overtook Bret Meyer to take the record for most passing yards and touchdowns in Iowa State history. In a 41–38 defeat over Texas Tech, he ran for 42 yards and a score in addition to throwing for 307 yards and two touchdowns. 81 throwing touchdowns and 12,170 passing yards were his final collegiate stats.

Brock Purdy

These are some of Brock Purdy's best college football moments. He is now making his impact in the NFL after being one of Iowa State's most successful and prolific quarterbacks in history.

CHAPTER 4 : RISING STAR AT IOWA STATE

The incredible narrative of Brock Purdy's ascent to fame at Iowa State is one of skill, chance, and tenacity. He developed into one of college football's top quarterbacks and the San Francisco 49ers selected him in the draft.

Purdy was a three-star prospect out of Arizona who had offers from Texas A&M and Alabama, two of the Power Five colleges. Nonetheless, he thought Iowa State was the best fit for him and that he could contribute right away, so he decided to go. In 2018, Purdy played his first game as a freshman and helped the Cyclones pull off an incredible upset against Oklahoma State. Along with running for a score, he completed 318 yards of passing for four touchdowns. In addition to winning the starting position for the remainder of the season, he was awarded the Big 12 Newcomer of the Week.

As a sophomore in 2019, Purdy kept up his impressive play, establishing school records for touchdowns (27) and passing yards (3,982) in a single season. In addition, he was the national leader in completions (312) and total offence (4,231) rankings. He was chosen for the second team of the Big 12 and was a semifinalist for the Davey O'Brien Award, which is presented to the finest quarterback in the country.

In 2020, Purdy had yet another outstanding season as a junior, helping Iowa State win a bowl game and make its first trip to the Big 12 Championship Game. A school record 66.6 percent of his throws were completed, and he finished 2,750 yards of passing with 19 touchdowns. He earned the Fiesta Bowl Offensive MVP and was selected to the first team of the Big 12. Along with being a second-team Academic All-American, he was also a semifinalist for the Manning Award and the Davey O'Brien Award.

In 2021, Purdy came back to finish as Iowa State's senior and try to win the Big 12 and make it to the College Football Playoffs for the first time. With a career-high completion percentage of 71.7 percent, he completed 3188 yards of passing with 19 touchdowns. He became the most successful quarterback in program history (30-17) and the all-time leader in passing yards (12,170) and touchdowns (81).

He was named to the AP's first team All-Big 12 and second team Academic All-American.

Brock Purdy had an incredible journey of growth and achievement throughout his time in college. Iowa State was always the underdog, but under his leadership, they became a national power and a conference challenger. He was regarded as one of the most effective and prolific quarterbacks in college football history, and his teammates, coaches, and fans all held him in high regard. Now that he is a 49ers player, he wants to leave his imprint on the NFL.

Breakout performances

In the 2023 NFL season, Brock Purdy, a quarterback for the San Francisco 49ers, has been performing incredibly well. He was selected as the last choice in the seventh round of the 2022 NFL draft, gaining the moniker "Mr. Irrelevant". He has guided his club to a 10-3 record and a postseason spot, leading the league in several passing metrics, therefore he has shown he is everything from inconsequential. Several of his standout efforts during the 2023 regular season are included below:

1. **Week 1 vs. Detroit Lions :** The 49ers defeated the Lions 41-17 thanks to a first-career start from Purdy, who passed for 314 yards and four touchdowns with no interceptions. With a passer rating of 156.3 the greatest by a rookie in NFL history he completed 23 of 28 attempts (82.1%). In addition, on four carries, he gained 28 yards and a score.

2. **Week 5 vs. Arizona Cardinals :** Purdy defeated the 2022 MVP Kyler Murray in an exciting 34-31 win against the Cardinals. With one interception, he completed 27 of 35 throws (77.1%) for 357 yards and three touchdowns. In addition, on six tries, he ran for 46 yards and a score. With 12 seconds remaining in the fourth quarter, he hit Deebo Samuel with the game-winning touchdown throw.

3. **Week 9 vs. Green Bay Packers :** Purdy avenged the 49ers' 2022 NFC Championship Game defeat to the Packers by passing for 328 yards and two touchdowns in a 27-20 victory

that included no interceptions. With a 136.4 passer rating, he completed 25 of 32 throws, or 78.1 percent of them. On five carries, he also scrambled for 37 yards. The longest play of his career, a 75-yard touchdown pass with George Kittle in the third quarter, was the result of his connection.

4. Week 14 vs. Seattle Seahawks : In a 28-16 victory against the division-rival Seahawks, Purdy threw for a career-high 368 yards and two touchdowns while picking up no interceptions. He had a 131.8 passer rating and completed 29 of 38 passes (76.3%). He also made three efforts at 21 yards of running. In the first quarter, he found Samuel for a 43-yard touchdown throw, and in the fourth quarter, he found Kittle for a 15-yard touchdown pass.

These are just a few instances of Purdy's amazing performances. In only his second season in the league, he has already gained the respect and admiration of coaches, fans, and teammates with his incredible composure, accuracy, and leadership. He has a promising future ahead of him and is a great contender for the MVP award.

Recognition and accolades received

The 49ers chose Brock Purdy as their last choice in the 2022 NFL Draft, making him Mr. Irrelevant for that particular year. But he showed his value in 2023, when he led the 49ers to two straight division victories and a Pro Bowl candidacy.

Purdy has won many honours and recognitions throughout his time in academia and the workplace, including:

- 2023 NFL passing rating leader
- Pro Bowl participant (2023)
- 2022 PFWA All-Rookie Squad
- Sportsman of the Year, Big 12 (2022)
- Leading Group Coaches (2020)
- All-Big 12; AP (2021)
- 2019's Second Team All-Big 12
- Gatorade Player of the Year in Arizona, 2017

In addition, Purdy owns a number of 49ers and Iowa State records, including:

- The most passing yards a 49ers quarterback has ever had in a single season (5,654 in 2023)
- The most number of throwing touchdowns (27 in 2019) scored by an Iowa State quarterback in one season.
- Iowa State quarterback with the most passing yards in a single game (510 vs Oklahoma State in 2019)
- An Iowa State quarterback's highest total touchdown total in a single game (6 against West Virginia in 2018)

Purdy is regarded as a rising star in the NFL and one of the greatest quarterbacks in the game. In addition, he's a contender for the AP 2023 NFL MVP title.

CHAPTER 5 :
CHALLENGES AND
TRIUMPHS

The quarterback for the NFL's San Francisco 49ers is Brock Purdy. Throughout his career, he has triumphed against several obstacles both on and off the field.

Purdy was selected with the 255th overall selection in the seventh round of the 2021 NFL draft. He was dubbed "Mr. Irrelevant" since he was the last player chosen. His lack of stature, arm power, and experience at a big collegiate program made him an easy target for many teams to pass on. His team, Iowa State, isn't exactly renowned for turning out NFL quarterbacks.

Purdy was not deterred by his draft status. It gave him the drive to disprove those who doubted him. Under the direction of coach Kyle Shanahan, he put a lot of effort into learning the 49ers' intricate offence, and his composure, accuracy, and confidence won over both coaches and players. Also, he became close to his receivers, particularly tight end George

Kittle, who turned into one of his favourite targets.

In Week 4 of the 2021 season, Purdy was given the opportunity to start after Jimmy Garoppolo's season-ending injury sustained by the 49ers. With a 12-4 record, Purdy grabbed the 49ers' NFC West division championship and the number one seed in the NFC playoffs. With a passing rating of 104.7, he completed his passes for 3,789 yards, 28 touchdowns, and only seven interceptions. He received his first selection to the Pro Bowl and was awarded the NFL Offensive Rookie of the Year.

During the playoffs, Purdy demonstrated his leadership and resiliency as well. He overcame a poor start to lead the 49ers to a 24-21 comeback victory against the Green Bay Packers in the NFC divisional playoffs. With 1:12 remaining in the game, he threw Kittle the game-winning touchdown pass. He outperformed Matthew Stafford of the Detroit Lions in the NFC championship game, passing for 326 yards and three touchdowns in a 31-17 triumph. Being his team's first-ever rookie quarterback to win a Super Bowl, he made history.

In Super Bowl LVI, Purdy's greatest victory came against the reigning champion Kansas City Chiefs and their standout quarterback, Patrick Mahomes. The 49ers won 34–31 thanks to a touchdown from Purdy, who matched Mahomes pass for throw. This was the team's sixth Super Bowl triumph and first since 1995. Purdy ran for a score in addition to throwing for 287 yards and two scores.

Despite his on-field achievements, Purdy had personal difficulties. He had to contend with the expectations of a devoted fan following as well as the strain and criticism that come with being the face of a legendary franchise. Purdy donned his father's initials on his helmet and dedicated his season to him. He said that his father was the source of all of his motivation and encouragement and that he could feel him in every game.

Purdy's tale is one of triumphing over hardship, going against the grain, and reaching greatness. He has established himself as one of the NFL's top young quarterbacks, winning the respect and affection of teammates, coaches, and supporters alike. In addition, he has grown to be a symbol of hope and inspiration for many others who experience comparable difficulties in life. He has shown that anything is achievable if one has faith, perseverance, and hard effort.

Overcoming Obstacles In Purdy's journey

The San Francisco 49ers quarterback Brock Purdy is an incredible player in the NFL. Mr. Irrelevant, as he was dubbed, was the last player chosen in the 2022 selection. He has guided the 49ers to six straight victories and a postseason spot, however, making history as the lowest-drafted rookie to start and win an NFL playoff game. He has shown that he is anything from inconsequential.

Purdy's path to fame was not a simple one. Despite being a standout athlete at Perry High School in Arizona, he had several difficulties and setbacks along the road. Most college recruiters ignored him. Iowa State was the only Power Five school to offer him a scholarship, which he ultimately accepted.

Being forced to fight for the starting position at Iowa State, where he was the backup quarterback at first. Due to injuries to the first two quarterbacks, he was given the opportunity to play as a freshman. He took advantage of the chance and guided the Cyclones to an 8-4 record, breaking many school records in the process.

His effectiveness and draft value were impacted by dealing with injuries and inconsistency throughout his junior and senior seasons at Iowa State. In 2020, he had a high ankle injury that impairs his range of motion. Along with struggling to adjust to a new offensive scheme, he also threw more interceptions than touchdowns in 2021.

Drafted by the 49ers in the seventh round, he was anticipated to be the backup quarterback to Jimmy Garoppolo and Trey Lance, the third overall choice in the 2021 draft. His work ethic and leadership pleased the coaches and teammates throughout the preseason and practice squad, when he had to establish himself.

Taking up the starting position in December with the injuries to Lance and Garoppolo. He had to lead a great but injury-plagued team to the playoffs, which meant he was under tremendous pressure and expectation. With only three interceptions in seven games, he passed for 16 touchdowns and showed incredible accuracy, composure, and confidence.

Purdy's determination, passion, and glory are evident in his ability to overcome these challenges. He has overcome the obstacles to establish himself as one of the NFL's most captivating and motivational players. With a chance to become the first rookie quarterback to win a Super Bowl, he can create history. He embodies the saying, "It's not how you start, it's how you finish."

MEMORABLE VICTORIES

He was the 2022 NFL Draft Mr. Irrelevant after being chosen by the 49ers with the last choice, when he was a collegiate football player for the Iowa State Cyclones. Here are a few of his career's noteworthy triumphs:

1. **Oklahoma State at Iowa State, 2018**: In Stillwater, Purdy led the Cyclones to an unexpected 48–42 victory against the No. 25 Cowboys in his first career start. In addition to running for 84 yards and a touchdown, he completed 18 of 23 throws for 318 yards and

four touchdowns. Because of his efforts, he was awarded the Big 12 Newcomer of the Week.

2. **Iowa State vs. West Virginia, 2020**: The Cyclones crushed the No. 15 Mountaineers 42–6 in Ames thanks to a career-high 475 yards and three touchdowns from Purdy, who also added a touchdown on the run. In addition to being the first player in Big 12 history to have three games with at least 400 passing yards and three passing touchdowns, he shattered the school record for most passing yards in a game.

3. **San Francisco vs. Seattle, 2022** : Purdy replaced the injured Trey Lance in the second quarter of Week 14 to make his NFL debut. With 1:12 remaining in the game, he completed a 237-yard pass for two touchdowns, including the game-winning 76-yard pass to Deebo Samuel, which propelled the 49ers to a 31-28 victory against the Seahawks. He was named the NFC Offensive Player of the Week.

4. **Green Bay at San Francisco, 2023** : At Lambeau Field, Purdy completed 23 of 39 passes for 252 yards, one touchdown, and no interceptions as the 49ers defeated the Packers

24–21 in the divisional round. In the last drive, he also ran for 27 yards and made a critical fourth-and-1 conversion with a sneak, which set up Robbie Gould's game-winning 45-yard field goal as time ran out.

CHAPTER 6 : IMPACT ON THE TEAM

Originally from Phoenix, Iowa State is where Brock Purdy played collegiate football. Purdy has shown to be a useful and effective leader for the 49ers, who are currently one victory away from winning the Super Bowl, despite being disregarded and underestimated by many pundits and fans.

Purdy has had a multifaceted influence on the 49ers. As a quarterback, he has shown exceptional accuracy and efficiency, topping the NFL in a number of statistical categories including completion %, yards per attempt, yards per pass completion, and passer rating. In the regular season, he has also completed 41 touchdown passes for 4,280 yards and only 11 interceptions. By passing the ball to different playmakers like Deebo Samuel, Brandon Aiyuk, and George Kittle, Purdy has shown that he can function in Kyle Shanahan's offence.

Purdy has shown to have a clutch and resilient attitude in pivotal situations. Throughout the regular season, he has guided the 49ers to four fourth-quarter comebacks and five game-winning drives. In Week 18, he led the team to a thrilling victory against the Los Angeles Rams, which guaranteed them a postseason place. A stunning victory against the Green Bay Packers in the divisional round, when he masterminded a late game-winning drive to overcome a 21-14 deficit, was only one of his three playoff victories.

Coaches, players, and the media have all shown their love and affection for Purdy, and they have stood up for him in the face of persistent criticism and defamation from some areas. Purdy has raised the bar for everyone around him and proven his sceptics wrong by using his own drive and the grudge he carries around with him. As their quarterback, his teammates have embraced him and applauded his work ethic, leadership, and self-assurance.

The 49ers, who are now among the favourites to win the Super Bowl, have greatly benefited from Brock Purdy. In addition to overcoming the difficulties and setbacks he has had during his career, he has shown his abilities, composure, and character as a quarterback. As the first Mr. Irrelevant to lead his club to the conference title game, Purdy has not only established himself as a prominent figure in the

NFL but also in history. The amazing tale of Purdy shows how persistence, hard effort, and faith can pay off.

Purdy's leadership qualities

One NFL quarterback that is a member of the 49ers is Brock Purdy. Although he was selected with the last choice in the 2022 NFL Draft, he has shown that he is a capable leader both on and off the field. Three adjectives may be used to describe Purdy's leadership style: resilience, humility, and confidence.

Purdy maintains a low profile while discussing his accomplishments and team position. In addition to not being haughty or rude toward his rivals, he does not allow his success to go to his head. Acknowledging his faults and limitations, he is constantly willing to learn from his instructors and teammates. He recognizes the work of all those involved and does not claim credit for the team's victories. Though it keeps him grounded and focused, Purdy's humility is valued by both his colleagues and his fans.

Purdy has self-assurance in his skills and future. Putting his faith in his own abilities and work ethic, he refuses to allow his draft status or his detractors define him. His confidence in himself and his team is evident, and he is not scared to take chances or make significant plays. He encourages his teammates to play with the same mentality by projecting confidence in the huddle, the locker room, and the field. Purdy has an infectious confidence that enables him to excel in his performance.

In the face of hardship and difficulties, Purdy demonstrates resilience. He takes chances to learn and get inspiration from losses and injuries rather than letting them stop him. He has the ability to pick himself up after failures and blunders, and he prefers to concentrate on the play that is now taking place rather than thinking about the past or the future. Pressure and expectations are not able to break him, and he remains unaffected by outside noise. Purdy's incredible tenacity serves him well as he guides his squad to triumph.

Humility, confidence, and resilience characterise Brock Purdy as a leader. His professional success and the respect and affection of his teammates, coaches, and the media have all been facilitated by these attributes. Being active in several humanitarian and social issues, Purdy is not only a leader in the locker room but also in the community. As a significant member of the 49ers, Purdy serves as an inspiration for upcoming leaders and young athletes.

CHAPTER 7: PERSONAL GROWTH AND DEVELOPMENT

After a stellar Iowa State career, Brock Purdy was selected as the last choice in the seventh round of the 2022 NFL Draft. Gilbert, Arizona, native Purdy attended Perry High School, where he won the 2017–18 Arizona Football Player of the Year award. During his time in high school, he passed for 8,937 yards and 107 touchdowns.

In 2018, Purdy, a three-star prospect, committed to Iowa State. Although it was anticipated that he would redshirt his first year, he was able to participate since the starter was injured. In eight games as a starter, he passed for 2,250 yards and sixteen touchdowns.

In his second season, Purdy took over as the Cyclones' full-time starter and guided them to a 7-6 record and a bowl trip. In a single season, he broke the school records for throwing yards (3,982), completions (312), and total offence (4,231). In his junior and senior years, Purdy made even more progress, helping

Iowa State defeat Oregon in the Fiesta Bowl and get to the Big 12 Championship Game twice in a row. At the end of his collegiate career, he held the records for most throwing yards (12,170), touchdowns (81), and victories (28).

Purdy received recognition for his academic success, community involvement, and sportsmanship as well. In addition to participating in several activities and organisations including the Fellowship of Christian Athletes, Night to Shine, Victory Day, and the Boys & Girls Club, he was selected the Big 12 Sportsman of the Year for 2021–2022. The 49ers selected Purdy with the 262nd and last choice in the 2022 NFL Draft. Several experts questioned his chances of succeeding at the next level when he was selected as the sixth quarterback overall in the draft.

With an outstanding first year that saw him lead the 49ers to a 12-5 record and the NFC West championship, Purdy disproved the doubters. With only seven interceptions, his 3,764 yards of passing were completed with 28 touchdowns. In addition, he scored four touchdowns and 421 yards on rushes. In addition to making the Pro Bowl, he was voted the NFL Offensive Rookie of the Year.

In his second season, Purdy improved on his stellar rookie year by passing for 4,217 yards and 35 touchdowns against only six interceptions. In addition, he rushed for five touchdowns and 367 yards. The 49ers, who will take on the Detroit Lions in the NFC Championship Game, are 13-4 under his leadership. Purdy has credited his coaches and teammates, his hard ethic, and his religion for his quick progress. He said he strives to become better at every facet of his game and takes things one day at a time. He said that he ignores other distractions and concentrates on his team and his objectives.

CHAPTER 8: POTENTIAL IMPACT ON THE NFL

Purdy, the 49ers' last-round selection, has shown to be an invaluable asset, helping the team win two straight division championships and qualify for the Super Bowl in 2023. Given his impressive skill set, tenacity, and leadership in his brief NFL career, Purdy has enormous potential to make an impact.

Purdy had a difficult time getting into the NFL since so many NFL scouts and college recruiters passed him over. While a member of the Iowa State Cyclones football team, he established many school records and was named an All-Big 12 player. Nevertheless, he was expected to be a late-round selection or an undrafted free agent and was not invited to the NFL Scouting Combine. He was selected eleventh overall in the 2022 NFL Draft, behind more highly anticipated players like Trey Lance, Justin Fields, and Trevor Lawrence.

After Jimmy Garoppolo and Lance, Purdy started his NFL debut season as the third-string quarterback. Until Week 13, when Garoppolo and Lance both sustained injuries, he did not see any play. With three touchdowns and 314 yards passing in his first game back in the starting lineup, Purdy helped the 49ers overcome the Seattle Seahawks. In the four games that followed, he won each one and contributed to the 49ers earning the NFC West division championship. Purdy made the PFWA All-Rookie Team after finishing the regular season with 1,857 passing yards, 15 touchdowns, and four interceptions.

Purdy's great performance continued into the postseason, as he threw for 378 yards and four touchdowns while leading the 49ers to an exciting overtime victory against the Green Bay Packers in the divisional round. The NFC Championship Game was his next opponent, and he outperformed the seasoned quarterback by passing for 296 yards and two touchdowns to lead the 49ers to a 31-28 victory against Tom Brady and the Tampa Bay Buccaneers. Since Russell Wilson's 2013 arrival to the Super Bowl, Purdy became the only rookie quarterback to make it there.

Purdy and the 49ers took on the Kansas City Chiefs, who were vying for a third straight championship, in Super Bowl LVI. Purdy gave it his all, passing for 327 yards and three touchdowns, but the 49ers were defeated by the Chiefs 34-31. Many commentators and fans acknowledged Purdy's potential to be a star in the game after praising his play.

Purdy bounced back stronger in the 2023 season, demonstrating that he did not let the Super Bowl defeat break his confidence. With one of the league's most explosive attacks, he made a name for himself as the 49ers' uncontested starter and captain. In passing yards (5,654), touchdowns (44), completion percentage (68.7%), and passer rating (111.4), Purdy set four NFL records, all of which were held by the 49ers within a single season. The NFL record for the most straight games with at least 300 passing yards was also achieved by him (12). In addition to being a strong candidate for MVP, he was selected to his first Pro Bowl.

With a 13-3 record, Purdy and the 49ers were crowned the NFC West champions once again. After making it to the NFC Championship Game the previous year, they took on the Los Angeles Rams. The 49ers lost a close game 37-34, despite another outstanding performance by Purdy, who threw for 341 yards and four touchdowns. In spite of his sadness after the game, Purdy pledged to bounce back and help the 49ers win a Super Bowl.

Given that Purdy has improved and grown significantly in his first two seasons, there is no denying his potential effect on the NFL. He has established himself as the 49ers' franchise quarterback and a leader as the squad has grown to be among the league's most formidable. Purdy has also served as an inspiration to a number of young athletes who were disregarded or underestimated by teaching them that everything is achievable with perseverance and hard effort. Purdy has a bright career ahead of him at the young age of 24. He has the potential to rank among the NFL's top quarterbacks, if not the best of all time.

CHAPTER 9 : What's Next for Brock Purdy and the 49ers?

The quarterback for the top-seeded San Francisco 49ers in the NFC playoffs is Brock Purdy. Following the injuries to Jimmy Garoppolo and Trey Lance, he was selected in the seventh round of the 2022 NFL Draft and took over as the starting quarterback. With his outstanding rookie year, he helped the 49ers win a division championship and make it to the NFC Championship Game. Along with setting the team record for most passing yards in a single season, he was nominated for his first Pro Bowl.

Leading the league in touchdown passes, completion %, and passer rating in his second season, Purdy maintained his impressive play. Along with helping the 49ers win the division championship for the second time in a row, he also helped them earn the top seed and a first-round bye in the playoffs.

Purdy has hushed his sceptics and set up the 49ers to contend for a postseason run. He has shown that he is capable of handling the stress and rigours of the playoffs and leading the club to the Super Bowl, which has evaded them since coach Kyle Shanahan took over. Running back Raheem Mostert, tight end George Kittle, and wide receivers Brandon Aiyuk and Deebo Samuel are among his outstanding supporting group. His defence, which is headed by Richard Sherman, Fred Warner, and Nick Bosa, is also very good.

The Philadelphia Eagles, Dallas Cowboys, or Seattle Seahawks, the team with the lowest remaining seed in the NFC playoffs, will be Purdy's next opponent. He has a 4-1 record against all three of these clubs from his prior encounters. He must be ready for various defensive tactics and plans and steer clear of errors and turnovers. As the top seed and the greatest quarterback in the league, he will also have to contend with the elevated expectations and scrutiny that accompany that status.

It's evident that Purdy has the abilities, self-assurance, and leadership to guide the 49ers to the Super Bowl. From being a late-round draft selection to becoming an NFL great, he has triumphed despite hardship and injuries. He

Brock Purdy

has a promising future and the opportunity to
create history with the 49ers.

CONCLUSION: THE LEGACY OF BROCK PURDY

American football quarterback Brock Purdy was a member of the Iowa State Cyclones' collegiate football team from 2018 to 2021. He now plays in the National Football League (NFL) for the San Francisco 49ers.

Three-star prospect Purdy from Arizona decided to attend Iowa State instead of Alabama, Texas A&M, and other offers. Midway through his first year, Purdy took over as Iowa State's starting quarterback. He guided the Cyclones to an 8-5 record and an Alamo Bowl appearance. In his second year, Purdy shattered a number of school milestones, including total offence (4,231), throwing touchdowns (27), and passing yards (3,982). In addition, he was a finalist for the Manning Award and was named to the second team of the Big 12.

In 2020, Iowa State made their Big 12 Championship Game debut under Purdy's direction, however they were defeated by

Oklahoma by a score of six points. He finished fourth in the league in passing efficiency and was chosen to the first team of the Big 12 conference. In 2021, Purdy came back for his senior year and helped Iowa State upset Oregon 34–17 in the Fiesta Bowl to win the first-ever Fiesta Bowl in school history. He concluded his career as the Cyclones' all-time leader in passing yards (12,170), passing touchdowns (81), and total offence (13,347). He was once again chosen to the first team of the Big 12.

As the last choice in the 2022 NFL Draft, Purdy was chosen by the San Francisco 49ers, who made him Mr. Irrelevant for that particular year. After Trey Lance and Jimmy Garoppolo suffered injuries, he emerged as the starting quarterback in his debut season. Purdy led the 49ers to a ten-game winning run, a division championship, and a berth in the NFC Championship Game in 2022. He won all five of the regular-season games he started. With a passer rating of 109.6, he completed 15 touchdown passes and 4 interceptions in 1,789 yards of passing.

In 2023, Purdy remained the starting quarterback for the 49ers, helping them win a division championship twice. He also set league records for passing yards (5,654), completion percentage (68.7%), and passer rating (111.4). In addition, he got his first Pro Bowl nomination and broke the team record for most throwing yards in a single season.

The impact Purdy had on Iowa State's football team went beyond the milestones he broke. He turned into a role model for his colleagues and an inspiration to young sportsmen. His sportsmanship, perseverance, and work ethic set a high bar for others to meet. His inspirational tale transcends athletics and embodies the spirit of perseverance, unity, and accomplishment in the face of adversity.

Made in the USA
Las Vegas, NV
30 November 2024

13019894R00035